NICOLA KINNEAR

The Worry Bee

In an old tree, in a huge hive, the bees were getting ready for their day. Everyone was buzzing about, arguing (as they did every day) over where to find the best flowers.

Izzy picked up her bag and watched them, quietly. Some wanted to go this way. Some wanted to go that way. Then the door burst open and . . .

"You have to come **this** way!" cried a bee.
"I've found the most **amazing flowers** EVER!"

He wiggled and waggled and danced about, excited to tell his friends which way to go.

Then there was a WHOOSH! and a BUZZ! And everyone took to the skies.

Everyone except Izzy.

Izzy was the only bee who didn't fly. She was far too worried.

What if she couldn't do it?

What if her wings weren't strong enough?

What if she fell?

It all seemed too scary and dangerous. So Izzy did what she always did. She waited till the others had gone, and then . . .

. . . she walked.

That felt much safer. And it was nice going slowly. She could see all sorts of interesting things along the way.

There were snails having a race,

and grasshoppers playing high jump.

She'd miss all of that if she flew.

But walking could be tricky, too. Sometimes there were big cracks in the ground, and Izzy had to make a bridge to get across.

Sometimes she got stuck in a spider's web. **Yuck!**

But it still felt safer than flying.

And she had that amazing field of flowers to look forward to! She must be getting close – she could hear her friends buzzing nearby.

She pushed past some tall leaves . . .

"I can't walk across that!" cried Izzy.

If only she could fly! Her friends made it look so easy.
Izzy took a deep breath. Maybe it was time to try?

It felt very scary, so she decided to start small.
She clambered to the top of a big stone.

"I'll just try and fly to that toadstool," she thought.

But before she could jump off . . .

... the stone lumbered to its feet and walked away! Izzy was so surprised, she forgot to flap her wings.

She hit the ground with a BUMP!

"I knew I couldn't fly!" she cried. "I've come all this way for nothing!"

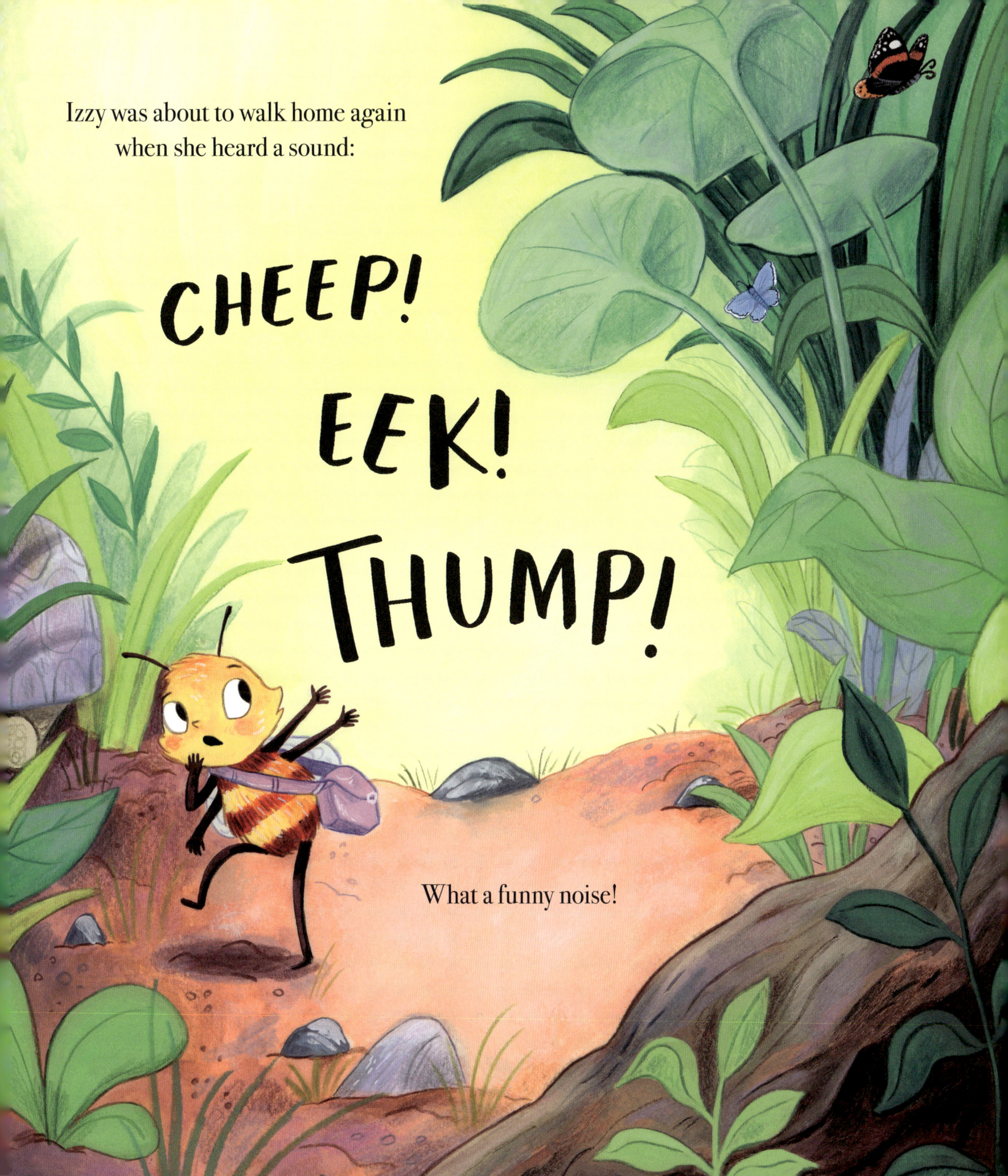

Izzy was about to walk home again when she heard a sound:

CHEEP!
EEK!
THUMP!

What a funny noise!

Izzy tiptoed round a tree.
It was a baby bird! It looked very worried.
"Are you okay?" asked Izzy.

"I was trying to fly," said the bird, "but I forgot to flap. Can you help me get back to my nest?"

Izzy looked high into the tree. The nest was a long way up.

"Bees are so brilliant at flying," said the bird. "If you show me how, I can copy you." Izzy didn't know what to say. How could she tell the bird she couldn't fly?

Then the baby bird squeaked: "Ooh, look at that big fluffy thing! I think it's coming to say hello."

A big fluffy thing? Izzy turned round and saw . . .

"Quick!" she cried.
"We need to get out of here!"
"Really?" said the bird. "How?"

"We're going to fly," said Izzy. "Come on. We can do this together."

"Flap your wings! Like this!" Then Izzy flapped. And the little bird flapped.

And they got higher . . .

. . . and higher.

"Look at us!" said the bird. "We're flying!"
"We are!" cried Izzy.

And they flew all the way up to the nest. "Thank you!" said the bird. "Flying is amazing! I can't wait to do it again."
"Me, too!" laughed Izzy.

And she couldn't remember why she'd ever been worried at all.

Then she zoomed off across the huge river …

. . . to the amazing field of flowers!

"Izzy! Where have you been?" cried her friends.

Izzy laughed. "You won't believe it when I tell you!"

Published in the UK by Alison Green Books, 2025
An imprint of Scholastic
Bosworth Avenue, Warwick CV34 6XZ
Scholastic Ireland, 89E Lagan Road, Dublin Industrial Estate,
Glasnevin, Dublin D11 HP5F
www.scholastic.co.uk

Text and illustrations © Nicola Kinnear, 2025
Designed by Zoë Tucker

Nicola Kinnear has asserted and reserved her moral rights
as the Author and Illustrator of this Work

HB ISBN: 978 0 702310 19 5
PB ISBN: 978 0 702310 20 1

All rights reserved.
No part of this publication may be used to train
any artificial intelligence technologies.

Printed in China

Paper made from wood grown in sustainable forests
and other controlled sources.

10 9 8 7 6 5 4 3 2 1

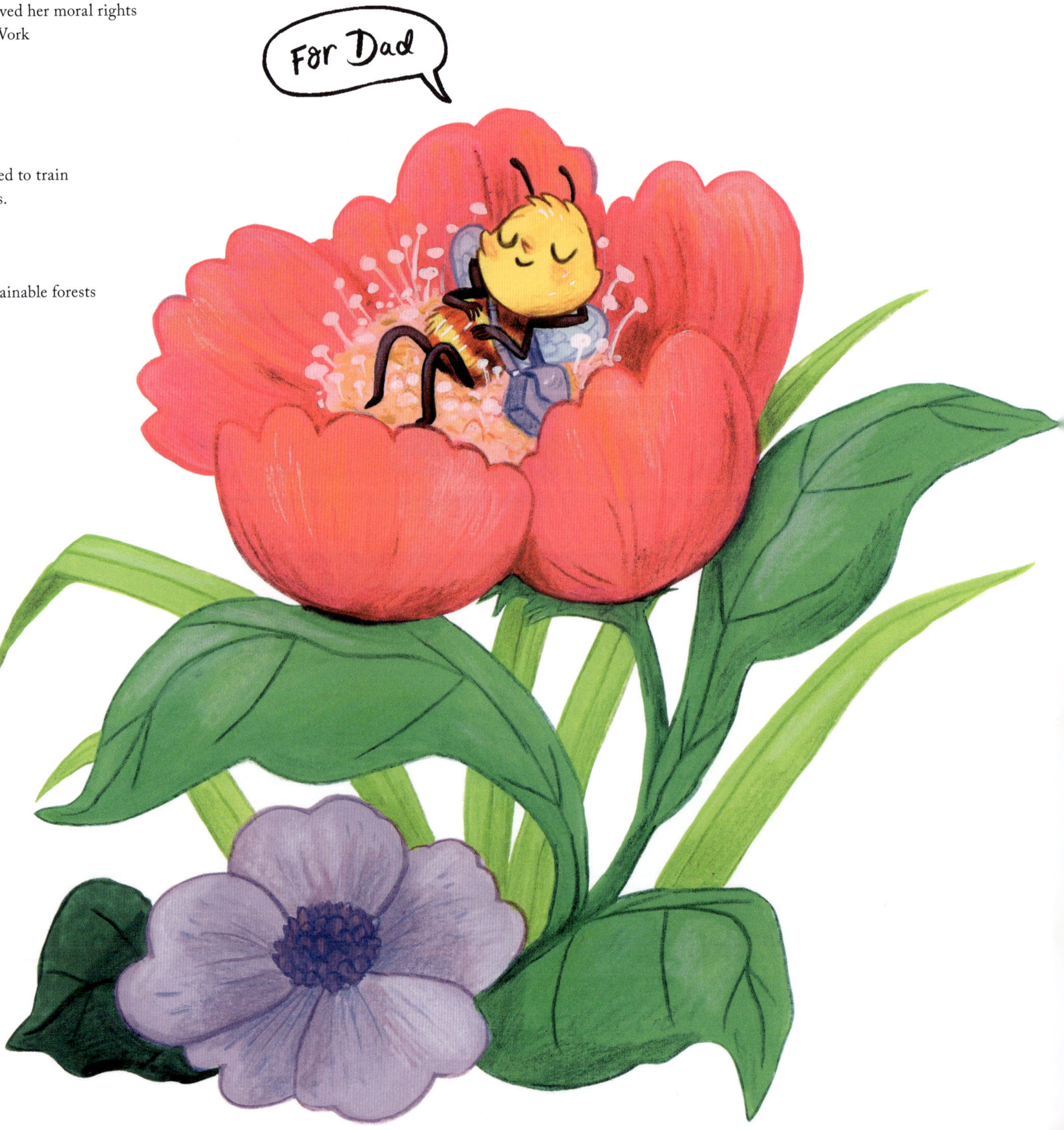